MW01615526

SPECIAL
DELIVERY

SPECIAL DELIVERY

COLIN WEBSTER

10 Publishing
a division of 10 of those.com

Copyright © 2024 by Colin Webster

First published in Great Britain in 2024

The right of Colin Webster to be identified as the Author of this Work has been asserted by him in accordance with the Copyright, Designs and Patents Act 1988.

British Library Cataloguing in Publication Data
A record for this book is available from the British Library

ISBN: 978-1-915705-31-0

Designed by Pete Barnsley (CreativeHoot.com)

Printed in Denmark

10Publishing, a division of 10ofthose.com
Unit C, Tomlinson Road, Leyland, PR25 2DY, England

Email: info@10ofthose.com
Website: www.10ofthose.com

1 3 5 7 10 8 6 4 2

CONTENTS

1

FINDING THE RIGHT GIFT

As a boy, I couldn't wait for Christmas to arrive. My older brothers and I would rush downstairs, eager to open our presents. But before doing so, we took it in turns to guess what was inside by examining the shape of the parcel, or by prodding and shaking it. We even tried to identify the contents by sniffing it.

After completing our forensic investigations, we'd announce to the others what we thought lay inside. Then we'd rip off the paper to see if we had guessed right.

Occasionally, this led to great disappointment. Especially when it really was – as predicted – a handknitted woollen jumper from grandmother. Although practical, this was not nearly as exciting as a football shirt! (Naturally, though, we still had to sound enthusiastic over the phone when we called grandmother to thank her.)

Finding the right gift at Christmas can be difficult, as the following story illustrates.

There were three wealthy sons who each gave their mother different presents they thought she would appreciate for Christmas. The first gave his mother a large house with substantial gardens. The second bought her a brand-new luxury car.

Then the third son disclosed to his brothers what he had bought her. He said to them: 'You both know that mother likes reading the Bible, but her eyesight is failing and she's finding it difficult to read. So, I've found her a parrot, which recites dozens of Bible verses, and he's been amazingly well trained.'

A few days after Christmas, their elderly mother wrote thank you notes to each of her sons.

To the first son she wrote: 'Dear David, Thank you so much for the house. Sadly, it's a bit too large, and I much prefer living in my small cottage.'

To the second son she wrote: 'Dear Jonathan, Thank you for the beautiful car. Unfortunately, my failing eyesight means that I'm unable to drive it.'

But to the third son she wrote more enthusiastically: 'Dear Donald, You have the good sense to know exactly what your mother likes – the chicken was delicious!'

I don't know who was more disappointed that Christmas – Donald or the parrot!

Although it's a struggle to find the right present to give someone, there is something deeply satisfying when the gift is precisely what the person wanted. Or needed.

The effort in sourcing the 'perfect present' is a sign of our love, especially when the gift costs us something personally. Indeed, when I think back to those handknitted jumpers my grandmother made for us, I realise the vast hours she put into knitting those beautiful jumpers (and they really were beautiful). They were an expression of her love and were exactly what we needed.

Tell me: have you ever viewed the first Christmas in this same way? That God loved you so much that he wanted to give you a gift which would be exactly what *you* needed?

The gift God gave would be costly beyond belief. But it would bring joy to all who received it. His gift was so important that it had to come via *special delivery*.

His gift was intended for everyone – including *you*!

SPECIAL DELIVERY

BY HEAVENLY POSTMEN

Nowadays, postal workers and delivery drivers wear uniforms, so you can identify which company they work for – whether it's FedEx, UPS or Royal Mail. Well, on that first Christmas, God sent his special delivery via a rather unusual postman.

Let me take you back 2000 years ago, to a stary black night on a hillside near the small town of Bethlehem. Shepherds were sat warming themselves around a glowing fire. They were probably recounting stories of which sheep had been mischievous that day and got lost. Or which one had narrowly escaped being nibbled by a wolf. When suddenly … the night sky, which had been peppered with the glow of a thousand stars, was eclipsed by an altogether different kind of light, and the entire hillside was floodlit.

The area shone not by light alone, but by a holy presence that accompanied it. From the perspective of the shepherds, it penetrated not only the darkness around them but also the darkness within them, for this light emanated from the glory of God. It was a glory so unimaginably holy and pure that the shepherds felt utterly unworthy to stand in its presence. No wonder they were terrified. God's glory does that to people!

Those shepherds felt so unworthy to stand beneath this divine spotlight of purity. But God's glory, rather than retreating from them, drew even closer. Indeed, it was precisely for those who felt unworthy and unholy that it appeared in the first place.

Then, from the midst of this dazzling display, a figure appeared. It was an angel of the Lord. I have no idea what the angel was wearing, but he needed no badge or uniform to identify himself. There was no doubt that he carried all the credentials of a heavenly being. No further ID was required.

And so, acting as God's heavenly postman, he delivered his message to the startled shepherds – a message of global importance, brimming with hope. It offered a peace so unique that it would calm the troubled souls of millions who would embrace it. The message was simple, but its significance was deep. The angel said:

Do not be afraid. I bring you good news that will cause great joy for all the people. Today in the town of David a Saviour has been born to you; he is the Messiah, the Lord. This will be a sign to you: you will find a baby wrapped in cloths and lying in a manger. (Luke 2:10–12)

As if one holy angel was not enough to frighten the pants off those poor shepherds that night, God decided to send a whole platoon! For the Bible tells us that a 'great company' of angels then appeared (Luke 2.13). And what's more, every one of those mighty beings could sing! They sang a refrain as if to reinforce the global significance of the Saviour who had been born that night and the peace that he would bring:

Glory to God in the highest heaven,
*   and on earth peace to those on whom*
his favour rests.
(Luke 2:14)

This was the first Christmas carol ever sung. And it was sung by representatives from another realm – heaven!

Why on earth did heaven send a choir? It could be because most cultures marked the entrance of royal visitors with elaborate fanfares and great ceremony. Yet, no such display was present to welcome the arrival of Jesus, the King of Kings. But heaven was not going to let the birth of God's Son go unnoticed by an uncaring world. So God provided the fanfare by means of this vast choir of angelic beings.

The message announced by the angels that night has echoed down through the centuries. Their words of hope and peace have brought comfort into the lives of all who fully understood their meaning. And they have lifted the burden from millions of hearts that were buckled by guilt and failure.

That night, 2000 years ago, God was sending a message to the world of such importance that it came by special delivery, via a heavenly postman – complete with a choir!

THAT TOOK A LONG TIME COMING

*I bring you good news that will cause great joy for all the people. **Today** in the town of David a Saviour has been born to you; he is the Messiah, the Lord. (Luke 2:10–11, my emphasis)*

I have a very good appetite. Indeed, whenever people invite us round for a meal, they ask my wife, Vic: 'Is there anything Colin doesn't like to eat?' To which she replies: 'Yes – small portions!'

Perhaps that's why Christmas dinner has always been the favourite meal of the year for me. The quantity and quality of food is especially pleasing. There is turkey, cooked to perfection – succulent and moist; and roast potatoes – crispy on the outside and fluffy in the middle; and carrots, peas and broccoli – all sweet and tender. And finally, that rich ocean of flavoursome gravy, bathing the whole dish with mouth-watering juices. Crumbs, it makes me salivate just thinking about it now!

I have to say that my mother-in-law cooks the most amazing Christmas dinner. However, one year we decided to stay at home for Christmas and I was tasked with sourcing the all-important turkey.

Now, I admit I had left it a bit late, because it was two days before Christmas and I still hadn't bought the turkey! Undeterred, I rushed to the supermarket and headed to the fresh poultry aisle. To my horror, every bird had been taken, with the exception of one small turkey (the size of a quail), which had an eye-watering price tag attached to it.

The Scotsman within me immediately had an allergic reaction to paying such an extortionate price for such a small bird. So, I wandered to the frozen poultry section. My heart sank – all the frozen turkeys seemed to have gone too!

Then I spotted one final freezer in which two birds were still left. Both were labelled 'extra large'. What's more, they were half the price of the small fresh turkey. 'Bargain,' I thought!

However, I use the word 'turkey' loosely to describe the birds in question, because to be quite honest, they were pretty much the size of an ostrich! And each had sufficient meat on the carcass to feed not just my family, but every family on my street – for a week! Undeterred, I heaved the vast block of frozen poultry into my arms (almost putting my back out in the process) and staggered to the checkout.

The queue was so long that I was beginning to suffer the effects of frostbite and mild hypothermia from clutching the frozen bird. However, it did give me time to read the label. It was then that I got the shock of my life. The cooking instructions said: 'Defrost this bird thoroughly before cooking.' It went on to say: 'This bird takes seventy-six hours to defrost and five and a half hours to cook!' I almost fainted. Why, that's half a week! By the time this ostrich is defrosted and cooked, I'd be welcoming in the new year, never mind Christmas!

Needless to say, I returned the frozen bird and reluctantly bought the extortionately priced fresh turkey. I knew the Webster household (and indeed my own stomach) couldn't wait half a week for Christmas dinner to arrive!

Let's face it – waiting is hard. Yet it seems to me that much of life at Christmas time is about waiting. Waiting in long queues at the checkout. Waiting for the first flurry of snow. Waiting for your loved ones to arrive home in time for festive celebrations. Or, children, eagerly waiting for Christmas day to finally arrive. Waiting just doesn't come naturally to us – especially if it's for something we have longed for.

So, imagine how those startled shepherds on the hillside near Bethlehem must have felt when they heard the astonishing message from the angel: *'Today* in the town of David a Saviour has been born to you; he is the Messiah, the Lord.'

'Today'! Why, that's like – *now*! Not tomorrow. Not next week. Nor next year. But right now.

That news broke the silence of centuries. Generations of God's people had been waiting. Waiting for the *special delivery of a special deliverer!* Waiting for the fulfilment of ancient prophecies, which said that God would send a Messiah – a Saviour. Waiting for someone who would liberate God's people from the power of their enemies. Waiting for someone who could set them free from oppression, bring peace, and God's kingdom rule.

God's people had assumed that God would send a great warrior similar to King David (who slew Goliath). Someone who would deliver them from the dark situation in which they were living, and who would restore hope, peace and prosperity to their nation.

For centuries their forefathers had longed for such a Messiah to show up and rescue them. But the years passed and no one came. Israel's history should have reminded them that God never fails to keep his promises, even though they may be a long time in coming. Successive generations hoped they would live long enough to witness the arrival of God's great deliverer. But heaven remained silent – until *now*!

Finally, the years of waiting were over! For that night the angels, acting as God's postmen, broke the silence of centuries.

The special delivery had come! God's gift had arrived!

The most important Christmas gift the world would ever receive was finally here. And it would be delivered in person.

SPECIAL DELIVERY

THAT CAME IN PERSON

YouTube contains some very moving videos of military personnel who surprise their loved ones at Christmas. Some disguise themselves as a delivery driver, hold a large parcel to obscure their face, then ring their parents' doorbell. Once their parent removes the parcel, they find themselves staring into the face of their son or daughter whom they thought was serving overseas. I confess that I need a tissue to watch those videos.

I also enjoy those videos where famous people surprise ordinary folk. One of the most amusing of these dates back to June 2022, when the UK was celebrating the Queen's seventy-year reign. During the broadcast, a BBC TV presenter interviewed Richard Griffin, the Queen's former police bodyguard, who accompanied her wherever she went.

Richard told of an occasion when the Queen, dressed in ordinary clothes, was out for a walk near Balmoral Castle (her royal residence in a remote part of Scotland). As they walked along, they encountered two American hikers and stopped to chat. It was clear they hadn't recognised the Queen.

The American gentleman asked the Queen if she lived nearby, she said: 'Well, I live in London, but I have a holiday home just the other side of the hill.'

The American tourist then asked: 'Have you ever met the Queen?'

Her Majesty replied: 'No, I haven't. But Richard meets her regularly.'

'Wow!' exclaimed the American tourists with excitement. And, quick as a flash, they pulled out a camera, handed it to the Queen and asked if *she* would take a picture of them standing next to Richard! The Queen duly obliged.

A few minutes later, the American tourists went on their way, utterly delighted that they had had their picture taken standing alongside Richard!

Little did those American tourists know it at the time, but they had just been standing in the presence of the most famous woman in the world – the Queen. But her royalty was veiled to them because she looked so – well, ordinary. Just like one of us!

In a similar way, when Jesus was born that first Christmas, royalty of the highest kind entered our world. But our world did not realise it at the time.

Jesus – who is the eternal Son of God, co-equal with God the Father and the Holy Spirit – took on flesh and became one of us. He entered our world as a fragile, dependant baby, who was born to a vulnerable young virgin girl called Mary.

Through Jesus, God was coming to us in person. Not in a vision, but in a body. And not in the body of a fully-grown man beamed down to earth. No, instead, he came in the developing cells of a human foetus which grew inside Mary, until the moment of his birth when Jesus took his first breath on our planet – as one of us.

As some of you are reading this, you might be thinking: 'Oh come on, you can't seriously be telling me that you believe in the virgin birth? I mean that's just not possible, is it?! How on earth can a virgin conceive a child without any sexual union?' Well, the truth is, it can't happen. It is utterly impossible. Yet, I firmly believe this *did* happen with the conception of Jesus. It is utterly unique. As such, it cannot be replicated. It is a miracle.

If you're sceptical, I sympathise because I used to dismiss Christians for believing such things too. And yet I'm now writing this book, so clearly something unusual happened to change my mind. And I hope the same realisation will change yours too.

Over the years, since becoming a Christian, I've spoken to several atheists who wanted evidence for God. One man said to me that he would only believe in God if he did something utterly impossible.

I replied: 'You mean, like the virgin birth?'

'No!' he said. 'Something else.'

'Well, what about Jesus rising from the dead? Would that be sufficient evidence for you to believe in God?'

'No, no,' he argued. 'It has to be something that we can actually get our head around.'

In other words, the only evidence he was willing to accept was that which had purely natural causes and explanations. Miracles were not allowed as evidence.

Friends, if God really does exist, then surely you would expect him to be able to do the utterly impossible – wouldn't you? You know, the kind of things that your head just can't get around. Things that go beyond the natural laws of science and nature. Well, if you're after evidence like that, then God has given us a whole book bursting with evidence – the Bible. It traces God's divine activity and dealings with humanity from eyewitnesses to those events. The virgin birth just happens to be one such evidence. It's the kind of thing that only God could ever do.

One piece of evidence that convinced me about the authenticity of the Bible was its predictive element. In other words, the Bible foretold future events hundreds of years before those events came to pass. For example, the virgin birth of Jesus was predicted by the Old Testament prophet Isaiah 700 years before Jesus was even born!

The gospel writer Matthew mentions the fulfilment of this ancient prophecy in his account of the birth of Jesus. He writes:

Mary was pledged to be married to Joseph, but before they came together, she was found to be pregnant through the Holy Spirit. Because Joseph her husband was faithful to the law, and yet did not want to expose her to public disgrace, he had in mind to divorce her quietly.

But after he had considered this, an angel of the Lord appeared to him in a dream and said, 'Joseph son of David, do not be afraid to take Mary home as your wife, because what is conceived in her is from the Holy Spirit. She will give birth to a son, and you are to give him the name Jesus, because he will save his people from their sins.'

All this took place to fulfil what the Lord had said through the prophet: 'The virgin will conceive and give birth to a son, and they will call him Immanuel' (which means 'God with us').

(Matthew 1:18–23, my emphasis)

Read that last sentence again, Jesus is 'God with us'! Don't miss the importance of it, like those American tourists did when they failed to recognise the Queen. This is an even bigger moment. Jesus is God with us. That's vast! That's immense! That's beyond our comprehension! But it's true. And it happened here on this planet. Our planet is the most significant in the whole universe because it was here on earth that God took on flesh and lived as one of us.

God entrusted his Son into the care of this young couple, Joseph and Mary, who nurtured him until he reached adulthood. Under Joseph's supervision Jesus learned his earthly father's trade as a carpenter. Think of that – there were tables, doors and ploughs which had been handbuilt by Jesus, the Son of God.

Now Joseph may well have shown Jesus how to build a boat. But I'm absolutely certain he never showed Jesus how to calm a raging sea from one. Yet Jesus did so. He commanded the very wind and the waves to 'be still' during a storm and the forces of nature submitted to the voice of their Creator (see Mark 4:35–41).

Joseph may even have taught Jesus how to make a coffin. But I guarantee you he never showed Jesus how to empty one at a funeral! Yet on more than one occasion, Jesus raised people from the dead. (You can read about these three separate miracles in Luke 7:11–17, Luke 8:40–56 and John 11:1–44.)

That kind of power – to subdue nature and raise people from the dead – doesn't come through human genes. You have to be God to do those things. And that's exactly who the baby born in Bethlehem was: Immanuel, God with us.

So, where would you expect to find such a precious delivery as this?

SPECIAL DELIVERY

LEFT IN AN ODD PLACE

With the rise in online shopping, many stores send their goods via delivery companies. But sometimes delivery firms get a bad press for failing to deliver the item to the right address, or for not delivering the item at all. That was the case for one postman in a remote part of Canada, who wrote at the bottom of his delivery card: 'I was unable to deliver your item because there was a huge bear at the porch door!' Personally, I feel that's a very reasonable excuse for not dropping off a parcel.

That aside, I was rather amused by a photo someone posted on social media of the calling card their delivery driver had left them so they could locate exactly where their item had been placed. The card had pre-printed options for the delivery driver to tick as appropriate and read as follows:

Hello, today I called to deliver your parcel. It was left:

With a neighbour (no tick)
In your shed or outbuilding (no tick)
In your front porch (no tick)
In your garage (no tick)

Having exhausted all possible 'tick' options, there remained a blank space at the bottom of the card for the delivery driver to write additional information to give the customer a sporting chance of locating their item. In that space, the delivery driver had sheepishly written the following brief, yet helpful, instruction – along with an apology. It read: 'Stuck on roof – sorry!'

A rather odd and inaccessible place to leave a special delivery, I hear you say. At least it was safe from thieves, bears and indeed the customer themselves!

But where would you expect to find a special delivery from God? Where would you place this kingly baby that had been promised by prophets and announced by angels? Surely this royal child would be born in a palace among princes. No!

What about the temple in Jerusalem, the place where God's presence on earth was said to reside? Wouldn't that be a fitting and holy enough location for a heavenly child to spend his first night on earth. But no!

In fact, Jesus' first night on this planet was not even spent in an ordinary home. Instead, it was spent in the company of oxen and donkeys, in what was most probably the barn section of a house. It's likely that the first air Jesus ever breathed that night was mingled with the exhaled air of livestock.

There were no comfortable, sanitised cots, or soft, fluffy pillows for this heavenly infant to lay his head. His first night was spent not in luxury, but in poverty. His bed was made of straw. His clothes were just torn strips of linen. His cradle was an animal feeding trough. It was just as the angel had told the shepherds: 'This will be a sign to you: you will find a baby wrapped in cloths and lying in a manger' (Luke 2:12).

And that's exactly where the astonished shepherds did find Jesus – in a manger. Perhaps that was the very sign that made their job of locating him so easy. In the small town of Bethlehem, there can't have been any other newborn baby placed in an animal feeding trough. It's certainly not the place you or I would have chosen. And neither would Joseph and Mary have chosen to place him there either. But they were desperate – because despite Mary being at the end of her pregnancy, they couldn't find anywhere else to stay in Bethlehem that night. No-one was willing to sacrifice their own comfort for them. No-one was willing to inconvenience themselves to make room for Jesus.

Someone once said: 'Jesus sought entry into the overcrowded hearts of those around him, but he could not find it.' Sadly, that's true even today. Jesus Christ is still searching for room within the hearts of people in the twenty-first century. But people continue to shut him out. They are too preoccupied with other things in their lives – things which they regard as being of greater importance and value than Christ.

They substitute God's great gift of eternal life, offered in Jesus, with man-made gifts that do not ultimately satisfy.

Today's world wants entertainment, not Emmanuel. They want consumerism, not Christ. They want Santa, not a Saviour. And so it is that people today continue to relegate Jesus to the margins of their life as an irrelevance, rather than valuing him as this world's greatest treasure.

The door of many a heart still remains shut to Jesus, just like at the time of his birth. The fact there was no room for him in the inn that night was symbolic of what would happen to Jesus throughout his entire life. Many refused him entry into their lives throughout his ministry. Sadly, the only place where room was ever deliberately made for Jesus was on a cruel Roman cross: When crowds gathered in Jerusalem and cried out for the criminal Barabbas to be set free from crucifixion and demanded that Jesus take his place.

On that day, Jesus died in the place of a rebel. On that day, the innocent died in the place of the guilty. But then, that is the very reason why Jesus Christ came to earth in the first place – to die in the place of the guilty.

Jesus came to save those who recognise and admit that they are not good enough to earn God's blessing. He came for those who recognise they have failed in life. The very thing that you would have thought should cause Jesus to turn his back on us – namely, our failure – actually drew him to us. Jesus came into this world to seek and to save those who were not good enough and who felt far from God.

SPECIAL DELIVERY

FOR THOSE WHO DON'T DESERVE IT

Perhaps you, like me, can remember being taken as a child to visit Santa in his grotto at a department store. I was only six at the time and, to be honest, it felt more like a visit to the headmaster's office at school. Once Santa had verified my name, he proceeded to interrogate me: 'Tell me, have you been a good boy this year?' he asked. And before I could lie (oops, I mean reply), he then gave the following ultimatum: 'I only give presents to children who've been good!' Gulp!

Isn't that what most of us have been taught? That Christmas gifts are only given to people who have been good enough and who deserve it? Maybe this is what led one little boy to write the following letter to Santa:

Dear Santa,

There are three boys living in my house. Jeffery is two, David is four and Norman is seven. Jeffery is good some of the time. David is good most of the time and Norman is good all of the time.

... I am Norman!

The truth is none of us are Norman. Even though we might think we are good all of the time, we have our faults and failings – like everybody else.

Of course, some people blame others for their failings. That's because we are living in an increasingly 'blame-free' society where we're always the innocent party, and never the guilty one.

Yet the reality is that we aren't blame-free at all. We are flawed and fallen people, who often make selfish choices. We want to be in charge and write our own rules – regardless of what God thinks. We choose to create our own morals and standards to live by, and ignore God's standards.

We are all rebels who live our lives for ourselves and for our own glory, rather than wanting to give glory to God. The Bible expresses it this way: 'All have sinned and fall short of the glory of God' (Romans 3:23).

Many people, on hearing that word 'sin', have an allergic reaction to it. They assume that it can't possibly refer to decent people like them. Surely, it's the kind of word one uses to describe despicable people, like criminals, murderers and dictators?

But we are not as squeaky clean as we might think, as the following illustration demonstrates. Once a preacher was traveling by train, during the middle of winter, to speak at a church in Wales. As he approached his destination, he noticed a whitewashed farmhouse building, which stood out in sharp contrast to the surrounding brown, muddy fields. A few days later, he boarded the same train and left for home. But the night before his return, a fresh blanket of snow had covered the ground, utterly transforming it. For as he gazed out of the train window, the preacher spotted the same whitewashed farm building as before, but what a contrast! Now the farmhouse seemed so dirty and grubby, in comparison to the dazzling white of the fresh, fallen snow.

Friends, when we compare our behaviour to that of other people in the world, like dictators or criminals, there is no doubt that we stand out as being quite good. Yet, what if the comparison was between you and Jesus? How does your life match up to his? How does your life match his faithfulness and honesty? How does it match up to his love and kindness? How good does your life look when it's placed alongside the perfect life of Jesus, who *always* obeyed his heavenly Father's will?

When placed alongside Jesus, even the best of us look dirty by comparison. Why, we can barely live up to our own standards, let alone that of a holy God!

Our lives are flawed precisely because we have veered away from God and followed our own agenda. God, the Creator of the universe, deserves to be revered and respected. His love and kindness towards us should cause us to be overwhelmed with love and gratitude towards him for who he is and for all that he has done for us. Although we can never match the depths of his love towards us, God is still worthy of our deepest affections and loyalty. But instead of loving God as we ought, we have loved and worshipped other things, like wealth, materialism, image and even our own popularity on social media – all of which are poor substitutes for God. In reality we are all worshipers – but we mostly worship ourselves, not the God of the universe. We all want to be mini-gods, in charge of our own little kingdoms. But our kingdoms won't last. Only God's kingdom is eternal.

Our failure to love, respect and follow God as we ought is not just disrespectful – it is high treason. And as a human race, we would all stand condemned before him, if it were not for one thing – God sent us a Saviour!

Remember the message that the angel announced to the shepherds: 'Today in the town of David *a Saviour has been born to you;* he is the Messiah, the Lord' (my emphasis). We need a Saviour. We need help from the outside, for we can never save ourselves. We need someone who can bring us forgiveness for our many failures. We need someone who can offer us a fresh start in life.

I once asked a man what he would like God to do for him. His reply was simply this: 'I wish that I could have the chance to live my life again and not do the things that I did wrong the first time.'

As we talked, I discovered that here was a middle-aged man who had deep regrets. He felt ashamed of aspects of his life – people whom he'd wounded through his words; people he had failed to love as he ought. I could see these sorrows were gnawing away at him. All he wished for was for his past mistakes to be erased. So, I told him the good news that God sent a Saviour who could do just that – and so much more.

Perhaps some of you feel like that man too. You may have an ocean of regrets and wish you could start your life all over again – with the slate wiped clean from your past. Well, my friend, there is good news. However many regrets you have, however distant you feel you are from your Creator, God has made a way for you to come to him for that fresh start in life. A life where Jesus is at the centre, offering you forgiveness and helping you become the person God intended you to be.

I believe God would say this to you: I came for the likes of you. I sent my Son for the bruised and broken people in this world, so that they might be made whole. I gave Jesus for those who have failed, but who long for forgiveness. I gave Jesus for those who feel rejected, so they might know a love that will never abandon them. I gave Jesus for those who feel worthless, so that they might know their true value to God.

Yes, Jesus came for the likes of you.

Thank goodness God is not like Santa! Thank goodness God's gift is available for those who weren't good enough. Thank goodness God sent a Saviour to rescue us and to offer us a new and eternal life with him.

But that would come at great cost.

SPECIAL DELIVERY

THAT WAS COSTLY

Around Christmas time, newspapers often print stories about what the rich and famous spend on Christmas gifts. Sometimes eyewatering amounts of money are paid for the most ridiculous of items.

For instance, a few years back *The Times* newspaper reported that the pet department of one exclusive shop in London was selling a fine china dog bowl lined with 22 carat gold, which cost £1,500. Not to be outdone, a Beverly Hills shop in America had a diamond-encrusted baby's dummy retailing at $17,000. That's mindboggling because every parent knows babies lose their dummies all the time!

Yet even the price of those items seems like small change compared to the spending power of the super-rich. For example, Mike Tyson, the world-famous boxer, bought his then wife Robin Givens a 24-carat gold bathtub for Christmas. The price? A cool $2.3 million.

You and I might stagger at the cost of those gifts. But even those mentioned above pale into insignificance compared to the price God paid to offer his gift to you. For it would cost him his son.

The enormity of the price God was willing to pay is demonstrated in the following story about a father and his five-year-old daughter. He took her around an art gallery containing many famous paintings and sculptures from around the world.

At one point, the father stopped to absorb the beauty of a famous landscape painting. But in that moment, he lost sight of his daughter, who wandered off. Naturally concerned for her safety, he began looking for her. Eventually he found his young daughter, who was staring transfixed at a life-sized marble statue of Jesus after his crucifixion. His lifeless form was slumped in the arms of his heartbroken mother. The pain and sorrow were visible in her face.

The little girl asked her father: 'Daddy, why has Jesus got a hole in his side?'

The father explained, as delicately as he could, that a Roman spear had caused the wound.

His daughter was visibly shocked that anyone could be so cruel. Glancing back again at the sculpture, she pointed to the figure and gasped: 'Daddy, there are holes in his hands and feet too. Why are there holes there?'

The father felt even more uncomfortable as he explained that Roman nails had been used to hold Jesus' body to a wooden cross.

His daughter's eyes widened, stunned at the awfulness of the thought. Then her small voice broke as she said: 'That must have hurt him so much. Why did he go through all that?'

The father explained, as best he could, that Jesus loved us so much that he was willing to die in our place and take the punishment for the wrong things we had done. He died so we could be forgiven.

The girl stood for a moment absorbing all her father had said. Then, approaching the figure, she slowly wrapped her arms around Jesus, lay her head upon his body and, in a quavering voice, sobbed two words: 'Thank You.'

Dwell on that truth for a moment. Jesus died for people like you and me – he suffered that agony for us. We have ignored God, broken his laws, lived lives without proper regard for him and deserved his holy judgement against our wrongs. But Jesus willingly laid down his life for *you* so that you could be forgiven and be reconciled to God. On the cross, the full penalty of God's holy judgement against our sin fell on Jesus, so that it would not fall on us. Jesus endured that agonising death because he loves you and wants you to be with him forever.

That's why Jesus came. To save us. To forgive us. To enable us to be reconciled to him. And to offer us an eternal life with him. And it is all a free gift! The Bible explains it this way: 'For the wages of sin is death, but the free gift of God is eternal life in Christ Jesus our Lord' (Romans 6:23, ESV).

Perhaps you can comprehend the concept of forgiveness. In fact, maybe you can see the immediate liberating benefits which that truth alone could bring to your life. But were you aware that, through Jesus, God also wanted to offer you eternal life too? For although Jesus died, he didn't remain dead. Three days later, he came back to life. His resurrection demonstrated that he had dealt the decisive blow to the power of sin and death and its claim over our lives.

Even to this day, there's an empty tomb in Jerusalem because Jesus walked out of it alive! And now he offers, to everyone who comes to him, a share in that eternal resurrected life. As Jesus said: 'I am the resurrection and the life. The one who believes in me will live, even though they die' (John 11:25).

By placing our faith and trust in all that Jesus achieved for us on the cross, we can receive a new identity as part of God's family. We can know God as our loving heavenly Father. We can have the power to live a new kind of life as we follow Jesus. And through Jesus we receive peace from God and the certain hope of eternal life with him.

This future promise of eternal life with God makes all the difference in the world to a Christian. It means that whatever life throws at us now and however hard our future circumstances may be on earth, we know that ultimately all our sorrows will have an expiry date. God promises that one day Jesus will return to earth again as

King and will make all things new. Everything that makes this world feel so broken and fractured will be fixed. God will wipe away every tear from our eyes, so that there will be no more pain, or sorrow, or suffering.

Best of all, we will be safe with God forever on a new earth. We shall witness even greater wonders and a more fulfilling life than this world could ever offer us. One even better than our best Christmas imaginable. And it will all be because of that first Christmas – when God sent Jesus by special delivery.

THAT NEEDS TO BE ACCEPTED

A few years ago, I read the remarkable story about a lady called Thelma Howard. She was an American maid who missed out on a vast fortune – all because she never looked closely enough at the Christmas present which her employer had given her.

You see, it just so happened that her employer was none other than Walt Disney, one of the wealthiest men in America. Every Christmas, Disney would give Thelma a Christmas card with a piece of paper inside it. Unfortunately, Thelma didn't fully comprehend what the piece of paper was, so she tucked it away under the mattress of her bed. Year by year, she received successive Christmas cards with the same accompanying paper, and the pile beneath her bed grew.

What's particularly sad about Thelma Howard's story is that she died in poverty. Yet, she needn't have. For after her death, her relatives uncovered various documents stored under her bed, including the pieces of paper she received from Walt Disney. To their astonishment, they discovered that these papers were in fact shares in the Disney Corporation – worth a staggering 30 million dollars!

Tragically, Thelma missed out on all the benefits of this vast fortune in shares. She had made the costly mistake of not bothering to find out what these pieces of paper really were, and had assumed they were worthless.

This is my appeal to all of you reading this book: please don't be like Thelma Howard, who missed out on the importance of her Christmas gift. Don't tuck the good news about Jesus under the mattress of your life. Don't just sentimentally glance at him at Christmas, then ignore him until the next year. I urge you to respond to Jesus today!

That's what the shepherds did when they heard about the birth of Jesus, the Saviour of the world. They ran to Bethlehem to see him – and their lives were transformed as a result. They returned to their work 'glorifying and praising God for all the things they had heard and seen, which were just as they had been told' (Luke 2:20). They took the joy of knowing Jesus as their Saviour into their everyday lives. They rejoiced in the peace and hope that Jesus came to bring. And all this was because they had responded to God's offer.

Important gifts are sent by recorded delivery. That means the courier requires a signature from the recipient, as proof the gift has been received. Well, God's intended destination for his gift to you is your heart. That's the place where we acknowledge our need of Jesus.

So let me ask *you*, have you ever thanked God for the gift of his Son Jesus? Have you received him into your life not just as your Saviour but also as your Lord, so that you are willing to obey him and follow him? If not, then what's stopping you from doing so now? Why not sign on the dotted line and make that commitment today, inviting Jesus into your life and into all of your tomorrows too. Why not begin that living relationship with him now.

The Bible says:

For God so loved the world that he gave his one and only Son, that whoever believes in him shall not perish but have eternal life. For God did not send his Son into the world to condemn the world, but to save the world through him. (John 3:16–17)

Below is a prayer similar to the one I prayed when I asked Jesus to come into my life and change me. I have never looked back since that moment, and rejoice every day in knowing the love, joy and eternal hope that Jesus brings to my life. Why not find a quiet place and pray this for yourself, and begin a new life – one with Jesus at the centre. If it helps, you can sign and date it:

Heavenly Father,

I have failed to live for you and have wronged you and others in my thoughts, my words and my actions. And I ask for your forgiveness.

Lord Jesus, I thank you for dying in my place on the cross, taking the punishment for my sins. I thank you that you rose from the dead and are alive and I want to receive the eternal life you came to bring.

I turn from everything I know to be wrong in my life and ask you to come into my life by your Holy Spirit. Help me live in a way that pleases and honours you.

Help me follow you as faithfully as I can, until you take me home to be with you forever.
In Jesus' name. Amen.

Signed: ....

Date: ....

If you prayed that prayer and really meant it, then that's *fantastic* news! You have just begun the rest of your eternal life with God. Jesus himself said:

> *Very truly I tell you, whoever hears my word and believes him who sent me has eternal life and will not be judged but has crossed over from death to life. (John 5:24)*

How amazing is that!

It's important that you begin to grow in your new relationship with God. So can I first encourage you to attend regularly a good church where the Bible is clearly taught? Maybe you were given this book by someone who is keen for you to hear about Jesus? Why not ask if you can join them at church.

Second, begin to read the Bible for yourself. You could perhaps start with the Gospel of Mark, which is a biography of Jesus. Or you may like to read a book called *Time Well Spent* which I wrote to help people get started in Bible reading and prayer with God. It's available from 10ofthose.com.

Alternatively, if you still have questions about Christianity, I'd encourage you to investigate further. There are helpful courses such as Christianity Explored or 321, which many churches run, that help people find answers to their questions. You can find churches running such courses by heading to:

christianityexplored.org or
speaklife.org.uk/321course.

Finally, I pray that this book will help you to encounter Jesus. May this be the first Christmas where you receive God's special delivery for yourself!

Happy Christmas!

You might like to read the words of this much-loved carol by Charles Wesley in the light of all that you have read.

HARK! THE HERALD ANGELS SING

Hark! the herald angels sing,
'Glory to the newborn King:
Peace on earth, and mercy mild,
God and sinners reconciled!'
Joyful, all ye nations, rise,
Join the triumph of the skies;
With the angelic hosts proclaim,
'Christ is born in Bethlehem!'

Hark! the herald angels sing,
'Glory to the newborn King!'

Christ, by highest heaven adored,
Christ, the everlasting Lord,
Late in time behold him come,
Offspring of the virgin's womb:
Veiled in flesh the Godhead see;
Hail the incarnate Deity,
Pleased as man with men to dwell
Jesus, our Immanuel.

Hark! the herald angels sing,
'Glory to the newborn King!'

Hail the heaven-born Prince of Peace!
Hail the Sun of Righteousness!
Light and life to all he brings,
Risen with healing in his wings.
Mild he lays his glory by,
Born that we no more may die,
Born to raise us from the earth,
Born to give us second birth.

Hark! the herald angels sing,
'Glory to the newborn King!'

More books from 10Publishing

Resources that point to Jesus

HOW TO SEE LIFE: A GUIDE IN 3D

HOW TO SEE LIFE A GUIDE IN 3D

Edited by
ANDY BANNISTER
GAVIN MATTHEWS

HAVE

Finding the Everyday Clues to

YOU EV

Meaning

WONDER

Purpose & Spirituality

TIME

A practical guide to
WELL
developing your daily devotions
SPENT

COLIN WEBSTER